THE
GOAL
MINE

PERSONAL SUCCESS SYSTEM

THE
GOAL
MINE

Personal Success System

SUCCESS SPEAKS
Global

THE GOAL MINE:
PERSONAL SUCCESS SYSTEM

Ordering Information:
Special discounts are available on quantity purchases by corporations, associations, and others. For ordering details, contact the publisher at the website or email address listed.

Website: **SuccessSpeaksGlobal.com**

Email: info@SuccessSpeaksGlobal.com

Success Speaks Global
2770 Main Street – Suite 147
Frisco, TX 75033

Printed in the United States of America.

How to Use the Goal Mine

The Goal Mine is designed to serve as a comprehensive accountability tool for the serious individual who is future-focused. This in-depth success system should be completed over the course of 1-2 days. *The Goal Mine* can be started at any time, but a new one should be completed each year.

Review each prompt carefully and write out several goals for each area. This process is not meant to be overwhelming. Record your goals for each item and set a target date for completion. Ideally, formulate a group of people who can work through the system with you and report your progress throughout the year.

Keep *The Goal Mine* with you for reflection and make updates as needed. You may be creative with colors, ink, markers, notes, or whatever personalizes the experience for you. This is not about making false promises to yourself or creating resolutions. Allow *The Goal Mine* to guide you through the steps to achieve personal success in every area.

I have personally used *The Goal Mine* to achieve massive results in my personal life, legacy, and business. I have also tested this system with several people who have reported positive progress and gained greater self-awareness after completing the process. It's time to "mine" your business. Let's focus and exceed our goals together.

Rekesha Pittman
The Goal Mine Creator

PERSONAL

GOALS

GOALS FOR
PERSONAL HEALTH

GOALS FOR
PERSONAL HEALTH

_____

_____

_____

_____

_____

_____

_____

_____

_____

GOALS FOR
SELF-CARE

_____

_____

_____

_____

_____

_____

_____

_____

_____

GOALS FOR
SELF-CARE

_____

_____

_____

_____

_____

_____

_____

_____

_____

_____

GOALS FOR RELATIONSHIPS: FAMILY

_____

_____

_____

_____

_____

_____

_____

_____

_____

GOALS FOR RELATIONSHIPS: FAMILY

GOALS FOR RELATIONSHIPS: FRIENDS

_____

_____

_____

_____

_____

_____

_____

_____

_____

GOALS FOR RELATIONSHIPS:
FRIENDS

_____

_____

_____

_____

_____

_____

_____

_____

_____

_____

GOALS FOR RELATIONSHIPS:
ROMANCE

_____

_____

_____

_____

_____

_____

_____

_____

_____

GOALS FOR RELATIONSHIPS: ROMANCE

FINANCIAL GOALS

GOALS FOR INCOME: WEEKLY

GOALS FOR INCOME: WEEKLY

GOALS FOR INCOME: MONTHLY

_____

_____

_____

_____

_____

_____

_____

_____

_____

GOALS FOR INCOME: MONTHLY

_____

_____

_____

_____

_____

_____

_____

_____

_____

GOALS FOR INCOME: YEARLY

_____

_____

_____

_____

_____

_____

_____

_____

_____

GOALS FOR INCOME: YEARLY

_____

_____

_____

_____

_____

_____

_____

_____

_____

_____

GOALS FOR MINDSET:
FEAR ELIMINATION

_____

_____

_____

_____

_____

_____

_____

_____

_____

GOALS FOR MINDSET:
FEAR ELIMINATION

_____

_____

_____

_____

_____

_____

_____

_____

_____

GOALS FOR STRATEGY:
DEBT ELIMINATION

_____

_____

_____

_____

_____

_____

_____

_____

_____

GOALS FOR STRATEGY:
DEBT ELIMINATION

_____

_____

_____

_____

_____

_____

_____

_____

_____

GOALS FOR BANKING:
MINIMUM ACCOUNT BALANCES

_____

_____

_____

_____

_____

_____

_____

_____

_____

_____

GOALS FOR BANKING:
MINIMUM ACCOUNT BALANCES

_____

_____

_____

_____

_____

_____

_____

_____

_____

_____

GOALS FOR INVESTING:
PASSIVE INCOME STRATEGIES

_____

_____

_____

_____

_____

_____

_____

_____

_____

_____

GOALS FOR INVESTING:
PASSIVE INCOME STRATEGIES

_____

_____

_____

_____

_____

_____

_____

_____

_____

GOALS FOR WEALTH-BUILDING:
5-YEAR GOALS

GOALS FOR WEALTH-BUILDING:
5-YEAR GOALS

_____

_____

_____

_____

_____

_____

_____

_____

_____

GOALS FOR WEALTH-BUILDING:
10-YEAR GOALS

_____

_____

_____

_____

_____

_____

_____

_____

_____

GOALS FOR WEALTH-BUILDING:
10-YEAR GOALS

_____

_____

_____

_____

_____

_____

_____

_____

_____

GOALS FOR WEALTH-BUILDING:
20-YEAR GOALS

_____

_____

_____

_____

_____

_____

_____

_____

_____

GOALS FOR WEALTH-BUILDING:
20-YEAR GOALS

_____

_____

_____

_____

_____

_____

_____

_____

_____

BUSINESS
GOALS

GOALS FOR
TARGETING IDEAL CLIENTS

_____

_____

_____

_____

_____

_____

_____

_____

_____

GOALS FOR
TARGETING IDEAL CLIENTS

_____

_____

_____

_____

_____

_____

_____

_____

_____

GOALS FOR BRANDING

_____

_____

_____

_____

_____

_____

_____

_____

_____

GOALS FOR BRANDING

GOALS FOR BUSINESS SYSTEMS

_____

_____

_____

_____

_____

_____

_____

_____

_____

GOALS FOR BUSINESS SYSTEMS

GOALS FOR
BUSINESS PARTNERSHIPS

_____

_____

_____

_____

_____

_____

_____

_____

_____

GOALS FOR
BUSINESS PARTNERSHIPS

_____

_____

_____

_____

_____

_____

_____

_____

_____

NETWORKING
GOALS

GOALS FOR MEETING PEOPLE

_____

_____

_____

_____

_____

_____

_____

_____

_____

GOALS FOR MEETING PEOPLE

_____

_____

_____

_____

_____

_____

_____

_____

_____

GOALS FOR
INCREASING INFLUENCE

_____

_____

_____

_____

_____

_____

_____

_____

_____

GOALS FOR
INCREASING INFLUENCE

_____

_____

_____

_____

_____

_____

_____

_____

_____

GOALS FOR SOCIAL MEDIA

_____

_____

_____

_____

_____

_____

_____

_____

_____

GOALS FOR SOCIAL MEDIA

_____

_____

_____

_____

_____

_____

_____

_____

_____

GOALS FOR TRADITIONAL MEDIA

_____

_____

_____

_____

_____

_____

_____

_____

_____

GOALS FOR TRADITIONAL MEDIA

_____

_____

_____

_____

_____

_____

_____

_____

_____

GOALS FOR APPS & TECHNOLOGY

_____

_____

_____

_____

_____

_____

_____

_____

_____

GOALS FOR APPS & TECHNOLOGY

_____

_____

_____

_____

_____

_____

_____

_____

_____

GOALS FOR HOSTING EVENTS

_____

_____

_____

_____

_____

_____

_____

_____

_____

GOALS FOR HOSTING EVENTS

GOALS FOR EVENT ATTENDANCE

_____

_____

_____

_____

_____

_____

_____

_____

_____

GOALS FOR EVENT ATTENDANCE

ENRICHMENT
GOALS

GOALS FOR
TRADITIONAL EDUCATION

GOALS FOR
TRADITIONAL EDUCATION

GOALS FOR
ONLINE EDUCATION

_____

_____

_____

_____

_____

_____

_____

_____

GOALS FOR
ONLINE EDUCATION

_____

_____

_____

_____

_____

_____

_____

_____

_____

_____

GOALS FOR
PROFESSIONAL EDUCATION

_____

_____

_____

_____

_____

_____

_____

_____

_____

GOALS FOR
PROFESSIONAL EDUCATION

GOALS FOR TRAVEL

_____

_____

_____

_____

_____

_____

_____

_____

_____

GOALS FOR TRAVEL

_____

_____

_____

_____

_____

_____

_____

_____

_____

_____

LEGACY
GOALS

GOALS FOR ACHIEVEMENTS

_____

_____

_____

_____

_____

_____

_____

_____

_____

GOALS FOR ACHIEVEMENTS

_____

_____

_____

_____

_____

_____

_____

_____

_____

GOALS FOR PUBLISHED WORKS

_____

_____

_____

_____

_____

_____

_____

_____

_____

GOALS FOR PUBLISHED WORKS

_____

_____

_____

_____

_____

_____

_____

_____

_____

GOALS FOR
LEAVING AN INHERITANCE

_____

_____

_____

_____

_____

_____

_____

_____

_____

GOALS FOR
LEAVING AN INHERITANCE

_____

_____

_____

_____

_____

_____

_____

_____

_____

GOALS FOR
GIVING & PHILANTHROPY

_____

_____

_____

_____

_____

_____

_____

_____

_____

_____

GOALS FOR
GIVING & PHILANTHROPY

_____

_____

_____

_____

_____

_____

_____

_____

_____

ADDITIONAL
GOALS

THE GOAL MINE
CREATOR

REKESHA PITTMAN
SUCCESS SPEAKS GLOBAL

Rekesha Pittman is called "The Midwife" because she has helped visionaries worldwide launch both books and businesses. Rekesha is in-demand as a speaker and panelist for a wide variety of topics including publishing, speaking, and entrepreneurship.

Rekesha produces innovative webinars, creative curriculum, strategic coaching, and successful profit-making strategies via online training, speaking platforms, live workshops, and group educational sessions.

FOR BOOKING AND INQUIRIES

SuccessSpeaksGlobal.com

Email: **info@SuccessSpeaksGlobal.com**

www.ingramcontent.com/pod-product-compliance
Lightning Source LLC
Chambersburg PA
CBHW051326220526
45468CB00004B/1515

* 9 7 8 1 7 9 3 0 1 1 6 5 7 *